From Darkness to Truth

ROWELLA JAMES

Copyright © 2015 Rowella James

All rights reserved.

ISBN-13:978-1516898978

ISBN-10:1516898974

DEDICATION

For Baby James

CONTENTS

Acknowledgments

Foreword

Invitation   1

Uniting Body and   5
Spirit

The Message   19

About the Author   129

Notes and   131
Reflections

ACKNOWLEDGMENTS

Thank you Victoria, for encouraging me to write this book, and also to you Gail, for rattling the cages and helping me to open my eyes once and for all to my true path. Eternal gratitude to Simon for showing me the Shadows, and to Katia for leading me ever further towards the Light. Finally thank you Claire for your lovely friendship and your invaluable help with formatting!

Written with special gratitude to Janet, who many years ago taught me to embrace the Shadow Self and to rejoice in the creativity and completeness which it would eventually bring as it became blessed with the Light of Truth.

Namaste.

FOREWORD

This book can be interpreted on three levels. On one level, it is a literal conversation between a spiritually and emotionally damaged man who is brought guidance and peace by a higher, spiritually developed other, who is referred to in this context as an Angel. On another level, the conversation between the man and the Angel could be interpreted as an

FROM DARKNESS TO TRUTH

inner dialogue between Ego and Soul, as the logical, socially conditioned mind both questions and seeks spiritual enlightenment. On a third level, it addresses the concept of human sanity, of the labels placed on individuals who are, at some stage of their journey, struggling to acknowledge, learn from and release the Shadows of their past and their present. Individuals who, with a little faith and guidance, can re-emerge in Truth as the pure, sensitive Light beings they once were, and to know that this way, too, is OK

INVITATION

Think with your heart about the dream which is truly harnessed within your Soul.

Shed the layers of the social Ego to touch the flame which burns within you at the heart of who you truly are.

This is the flame of life into which you were conceived. This is the flame of life which connects you with the deepest part of the Universe; the Source from which every form of life was drawn and to which it shall return.

In essence we never actually return or emerge, we simply are. A fragment of Universal Energy encased within a human form and carried within a Soul. When we truly stop to consider our potential we come to understand that, essentially, we have a real and everlasting Truth to which we owe our life's work.

If we can give all of our potential energy, dedicate our life's work to our Inner Truth, then we live in honesty and Love towards those around us, those who touch our lives from deep within and help to confirm whom we are; those people to whom we can dedicate a part of our mission in this life to help them fulfil their own Inner Truth.

The Source knows no boundary of faith, no cataclysm of religion or order. It is the infinite energy above and beyond all things on this Earth. The infinite Source is past, present and future for it has no concept of linear time. The Source lives within and around us, for it knows no separate energy, only that by which we are all inextricably bound.

The energy of Divine Consciousness is the energy within us all. The Source is within each one of us, therefore we are masters of our own destiny.

UNITING BODY AND SPIRIT

We are beings of pure, white Light. This light is our Spirit, the small fragment of Universal Consciousness which we carry within our physical form. When white light is shone through a prism, it splits into the seven colours of the rainbow: red, orange, yellow, green, blue, indigo and violet, each vibrating at its own frequency. In the same way, our Spirit is refracted by the prism of the physical body, into seven vortices of spiritual energy which work in unison with the physical body. These seven sources of vital energy are known as Chakras.

Chakra is an ancient Sanskrit word meaning vortex or spinning wheel. Although there are hundreds of Chakras within the body, we focus on the seven main sources of energy, which are situated along the spinal column from the perineum to the crown of the head. The Chakras store, generate and receive energy at the levels of both the physical and subtle bodies, *physical body* referring to the organs and systems and *subtle bodies* being our emotional and spiritual levels.

The concept of Chakras stems from the Indian philosophy of Ayurvedic medicine, the earliest records of which date back as far as around 2500BC. The word *Ayurveda* is a compound of two Sanskrit words: "*Ayur*" meaning Life and "*Veda*" meaning Knowledge. The Ayurvedic philosophy works on the principle that illness, be it physical, emotional, mental or spiritual, stems from an imbalance within these energy centres of the body. Ayurvedic practice brings alignment and balance through a combination of herbal, physical and meditative treatments.

Chakras don't exist in isolation from the rest of the body; on the contrary, each individual Chakra is an integral part of a holistic fusion of body, mind, emotion and spirit. However, the lower Chakras generally work more closely with the physical body, whereas the higher they fall along the spinal column, the more receptive and influential they are to the subtle body and the Higher Self.

In the same way that the Chakras drive and reflect our own life force within, they are also receptive to and affected by external energies, thus explaining why our well-being and ability to communicate can be affected by the mere presence of another person or within a particular environment.

Meditation is a powerful tool for tuning in to our Chakras and bringing them into balance through our own techniques of focus, visualisation and mindfulness. During this book, I will introduce you to a range of meditation techniques. Some you may love, others may not feel right for you at this time. Meditation is highly personal and as you come to practise more, you will find the things that work for you to bring you to a state of glorious, beautiful peace. For many people, meditation is shrouded in mystery, glorified as a perfect state attainable only by those few selected higher functioning individuals: a common misconception. Meditation is an accessible means for everybody to begin peeling away of the layers of protection and coping mechanisms which we create in response to our experiences in the earthly world, and which then generate responses such as emotions and fear.

When we meditate, we eventually become the essence of our own Inner Light. We penetrate the Ego and begin to touch base with the Soul. Eventually, we become the Universe. And as we are all flames of Consciousness within the same eternal Universe, we become each other, we become the oceans we become the stars. We join in union with the moon and we become the motion of the planet. We become intrinsically connected to the oceans and seas, the sunrise and the sunset.

Meditation does not always happen straight away. Like anything new or unaccustomed, we need time to adjust to it and take on board new sensations. We need to allow ourselves time to think about it, and to ask ourselves questions about it – and this is fine. To begin with, simply set aside 5 minutes to practise this exercise. There are so many different ways to meditate, but whichever method you choose is a means to an end. The true nature of meditation is to dip away from the superficial chit-chat of the mind, to transcend physical sensations and to touch base with your Inner Truth, in whichever ways feel right and accessible for you.

Your Sacred Space

Many of the meditations in this book will invite you to find your Sacred Space. This is the point at which you begin to transcend the chatter of the mind and experience a sense of peace and stillness; the point at which you begin to recognise a connection with your Higher or Spiritual Self. You may like to visualise your Sacred Space as a colour or an image or you may simply wish to feel and experience the sensations as they come to you.

Gnosis

Gnosis is an innate knowledge or spiritual wisdom which is carried within each one of us. It is the language of the Universe which calls out to us to follow our Truth and pull ourselves onto the path of our destiny. So often we fall into our predicted pattern of behaviour or make choices from the Ego alone. So often we consider and re-consider without realizing that the answer lies within our Soul. As you become better acquainted with your Higher Self, you will draw increasingly on your Gnosis by trusting in your inner voice and having faith in your intuition.

The Root Chakra (Sanskrit: *Muladhara Chakra*)

As its name suggests, the Root Chakra is situated at the very base of the spine in the area of the perineum. It is associated with the colour red and is linked to our base drives and survival instinct. When this Chakra is in alignment, we are grounded, secure and courageous with a general sense of energy, balance and enjoyment of life. This Chakra is connected largely with sexual rather than sensual energy and manifests emotionally as passion. In terms of the physical body it works in synthesis with the adrenal glands, circulation and bones – in other words, the foundations of the physical form and survival responses.

When this Chakra is out of balance, it can show within the physical body through symptoms of constipation, bladder infections and fatigue whilst at an emotional level we may experience feelings of irritability and aggression.

The Sacral Chakra (Sanskrit: *Swadhisthana Chakra*)

This Chakra, associated with the colour orange, is located within the sacral region and is connected to our social and emotional wellbeing. It is also connected to sensuality and fertility, therefore it works on a physical level with the reproductive organs. An imbalance of energy within the Sacral Chakra can reflect within the physical body as impotence, frigidity and difficulties with conception. As it governs our social and emotional well-being, an imbalance can also contribute towards depression, sometimes leading to drug or alcohol dependence to compensate for emotional security and love.

The Solar Plexus (Sanskrit: *Manipura Chakra*)

The Solar Plexus is located within the area of the naval, and is widely considered to be the power house of our physical energy. Its colour is a vibrant yellow, and brings with it a sense of purpose and security. When the Solar Plexus is aligned, we experience a sense of personal power, humour, mental clarity and joy. When it is out of synch, it can impact on both the digestive and nervous systems, whilst presenting at an emotional level as nervousness, anxiety and social insecurity.

The Heart Chakra (Sanskrit: *Anahata Chakra*)

The Heart Chakra, or Heart Centre as it is also known, is associated with the colour green. Physically it sits between the higher and lower Chakras along the spinal column. Subtly, it is the gateway between the physical and the spiritual. Balance within the Heart Chakra brings about a sense of harmony between mind, body and Soul. Meditation on the Heart Chakra stimulates a process of rebirth and healing and can bring about protection of the subtle body through visualisation and mindfulness techniques. This is the Chakra of compassion and love, and connects us at a higher and deeper level with other people, both directly and universally.

Physically, the Heart Chakra is associated with the functioning of the heart and lungs. An imbalance can bring about respiratory problems as well as mental tension. When we bring this Chakra into balance, it raises our level of receptivity to love and generates a sense of harmony, balance and peace.

The Throat Chakra (Sanskrit: *Vishudda Chakra*)

This is the Chakra of communication, healing and wisdom and is situated at the region of the throat. Its physical connotations are reflected in the neck, throat and shoulders and the ability to speak clearly. Over or under stimulation of the Throat Chakra can manifest speech disorders and tension or disease in any of these areas. Spiritually, the Throat Chakra allows us to speak our Truth both out loud and within ourselves. Blockages within the Throat Chakra can hinder our freedom of spirit and our connection with our True Self, which in turn can lead to frustration and mood swings as we fight the unnecessary battle between Ego and Soul.

The Third Eye Chakra (Sanskrit: *Ajna Chakra*)

This is our psychic Chakra associated with intuition, self-awareness, understanding and release, its colour being a deep, restful indigo. Meditation on this Chakra further deepens our awareness of the subtle body, enabling us to tap into the psychic energy which sharpens our intuition and sense of inner knowledge. When this Chakra is weakened or blocked, it can bring about nightmares, mood swings or bi-polar traits as our spiritual energy attempts to communicate through a domineering wall of physical energy. Within the body, imbalance of the Third Eye Chakra can manifest headaches and migraines.

    This Chakra generates the frequency of our auric field, which receives and transmits energy between other people and our surroundings, heightening our sixth sense. When it is low, our general energy level and awareness are weakened, whereas balance raises our levels of intuition and receptivity to the energy around us, be it our surroundings, other people or our heightened sense of synthesis between ourselves and Universal Consciousness.

The Crown Chakra (Sanskrit: *Sahasrara Chakra*)

This is our most spiritual Chakra, the violet peak of the Chakra spectrum. It is the source of spiritual harmony, meditation and mindfulness. The energy of this Chakra brings us into our Higher Self where we eventually become completely open and receptive to Gnosis. This Chakra is the one which we aim to focus upon during transcendental meditation as it raises our awareness of the fusion between ourselves and Universal Consciousness.

Misalignment can bring about symptoms of mental illness and a drive for material gain, which in itself brings dissatisfaction and breeds resentment, envy and contempt towards others. Balance within this Chakra takes us beyond the material, beyond the constraints of our Ego and creates within us a sense of mindfulness, deep fulfilment and leads us towards spiritual bliss. In other words, it awakens us to our essence, our purpose and completes the unity of the spectrum, revealing the wholeness of our complete and pure body of Light and Truth.

Grounding

Following any meditation, it is vital to ground mind, body and spirit in order to return to the day and to harmonise the Soul with your physical surroundings. Without proper grounding, we can end up feeling unsettled and disjointed from the events of the day and from those around us.

To ground effectively, we need to re-establish conscious contact with the earth beneath us and the air which surrounds us. During meditation, the intention is that our awareness is guided away from the physical body and into the realm of the Soul. Grounding requires us to return to the physical, bringing with us a gentle sense of peace and awareness from the higher frequencies of the Soul.

Visualise yourself sitting or lying on the Earth in your present surroundings. Visualise yourself breathing in and breathing out in your present surroundings. Gradually you will begin to synchronise yourself once more with the energies of the day. When you feel completely ready and it feels natural to do so, begin to feel once more into your physical form. When it feels right and natural to do so, begin to introduce some slight movement to your fingers and toes. Allow your breathing to liven. Begin to notice the sounds around you, connecting you to the earth. Now begin to recognise those sounds as part of your physical surroundings.

Feel the physical contact you maintain with the earth. Bring your hands to a prayer position and breathe here as the unity with your physical form increases with each breath. With your palms still together in prayer position, stretch your arms above your head as you breathe in the vitality of the day, pointing your fingers upwards towards the stars and the sky. As you breathe out, sweep your arms in a wide circle at your sides towards the ground, embracing the energy of your higher, spiritual Chakras and uniting them with the energy of the earth.

Place the palms of your hands on the earth and feel yourself grounding and completing your connection with the earth once more. Once again, visualise your surroundings; know exactly where you are.

Then when you are completely ready, and only then, slowly open your eyes and return with full awareness and gratitude to your day.

THE MESSAGE

PRELUDE

An Angel walked in solitude beside the waning day and asked the Universe to whom he should be drawn in order to make his peace with the Earth and beyond. The only answer lay within the very depths of his Soul:

> *"Seek not the one to whom you shall be drawn, but simply be drawn to the one with whom you shall this day belong".*

A man stands on the edge of a cliff, his back to the setting sun. Nobody knows he is there, not even the pulse of his own heart. All around his body, the air grows cold on his skin, yet he feels nothing but the Shadows in his mind.

Above him and around him, the first stars begin to press through the indigo sky, present for eternity yet visible only as the shifting of the planets allows, yet he sees nothing but the void in his life.

Beneath his feet, dewdrops are already beginning to gather like liquid promises of a new dawn but he smells nothing but the deadness of his spirit.

Far, far below him, the waves pound relentlessly on the rocks. This he hears like the relentless beating of his heart; the promise of sanctuary, the dream of peace; a finality that will envelop his Soul in velvet bliss and carry him to eternal, silent sleep.

At last. One step closer to his freedom.

The Angel saw the man, his body silhouetted against the fire of dusk. He saw the way the embers caught the outline of his form like a halo; saw the way the wind rustled his hair like a new leaf. Saw the way his physical form was enveloped in a deep, dark, impenetrable Shadow.

Slowly, the Angel approached him. He knew that the man would know. Like two Souls bound to meet, the man would be aware of the Angel's coming before he arrived in body.

In a premonition, a gentle nudge from the Universe, the man was aware.

"Speak to me."

And the Angel spoke:

"*Namaste*, my child, let me speak for the Truth is in being, and the being is the knowledge of an eternal force which drives us all. We are true Source and in denying so, we only serve the darkness. Reach towards the Light and shed the shroud of monetary life for we are entering a cosmic shift towards eternal energy; a synthesis between humans and Earth, water and fire, the ether and the profoundly real. The Source is within us all and we are all within the Source."

"SPEAK TO ME OF EGO AND SOUL"

"My Soul is dead. My mind is suffering. I am nothing more than the empty shell of a man, an ageing body exhausted by time."

"Our essence, our Truth, lies in the Universal Energy that is above, beyond, around and within us. Within each of us burn memories of the future, predictions of the past. So eternal, so boundless is this Energy which drives every fibre of our bodies, generates every reaction and moves every cell that it knows no linear patterns of time or physical events.

"The Ego is a transient shield which we build and create around us. We manifest Ego through our experiences in the human world. Through social expectations and the norms of our society, we create a barrier called the Ego, which protects our Divine Soul from conscious awareness. We create, more often than not, an Ego which protects us from the fears built up by our own minds, fears which we conjure in response to the actions of others.

"If we were all to live from the level of the Soul, then we would live in pure Truth. We would have no need for the shield of hope and vanity which the Ego provides. However, since we are living in a domino society where the actions of one person can shape the actions and attitudes of the next, we need our Ego to help us come through the day relatively unscathed.

"In order to find happiness within ourselves, we need essentially to work on integrating the Ego with the Soul. The Ego is not there with the intention of destroying us or to cause us pain. It is there to help us and to keep us safe. We use the mask of the Ego to help us repress the undesirable aspects of ourselves and to push them away into the Shadows of our subconscious, drawing a veil over them to shield them from our awareness.

"However, as our Light cannot be quelled, neither will our Shadows disappear; they will only be masked. Until we remove the obstacle which is casting the Shadow, we will continue to live at the level of the Ego while it works to defend us from darkness.

"We need to begin by thanking the Ego for all it has done for us to keep us safe throughout our lifetime. The Ego helps us to maintain social relationships, to function in our daily lives. It enables us to carry on regardless of negativity and to conduct ourselves appropriately. And while we are social beings here on planet Earth, it is important that we do function socially and appropriately - to a point.

"If we are not careful, the Ego can take over and try to lead us completely. It can attempt to shield not only the Shadows within our psyche, but also the Light which is the True Soul.

"In order to move forward and re-discover our Enlightened Truth, we need to gently move the Ego aside. We need to bring it into the Light so it becomes one with our Soul, and allow the Shadows to come to the surface to be blessed and released.

"When something is hidden away from the conscious mind, it becomes like the forbidden fruit – something more and more significant. Obstacles become greater, desires escalate and fears flourish. And the bigger these Shadows become, the harder the Ego has to work to conceal them. By constantly fighting against these Shadows, the Ego is providing them with more fuel. By fighting back, the battle grows and before long, we begin to lose touch with the Divine Light within, and instead are guided purely by the movements of the Ego.

"The Ego does not understand the Higher Self. The Ego is cerebral, and operates only at this level. The Ego knows limitations and is bound to situation and circumstance. We need to take the Ego by the hand and lead it to assurance that it is safe in the Light of the True Self.

"There is a common misconception that allowing our intuition – our Truth – to lead our decision making is a frivolous and irresponsible route to take: a butterfly existence. Another common misconception is that allowing the mind to rule will inevitably lead to solid, grounded, morally correct decisions.

"How wrong we can be.

"Our mind can only chatter about the things that the Ego believes to be true. Our mind is two dimensional; it can only see one side of the coin. It can only predict on the basis of a singular event within a series of outcomes. It can only infer on the basis of what the Shadows dictate and what the Ego believes to be true. However, the Soul is infinite. Our gut feelings, our intuition and instinctive understanding, that flashbulb moment of clarity are all moments of the Soul shining through.

"Living from the Soul is real and wise. Sometimes our intuition comes as a great surprise as many times our Soul lives in conflict with the mind. Our Ego protects us with false certainties about our lives and our desires. It is built of the messages we receive and the false interpretations which we make from others and in the end we come to realize that our entire superficial existence is built upon falsities and confused beliefs about who we really are. In order to overcome this we need to learn to still the mind. It is tempting to try to fight the flow of thoughts which come in and out of the mind, but by breathing deeply into the epicentre of the Soul, by acknowledging the Divine within us , we soon begin the detach from the mind chatter. It may not lessen in quantity, it may not change its tune, but it will cease to matter. It will cease to make an impact.

"The Ego can help us to discover and identify our Shadows. When we are prepared to really look at the way in which we behave and react, and the way it makes us feel, then we can begin to identify the point at which the Ego is taking over and from what it might be shielding us. As you connect to the deeper source of your Soul, you will begin to feel sympathy for the mind. It tries so hard to dictate and to lead, and to conduct life as it believes if should be. But it can only work with what it has.

"The Soul is a timeless bounty which knows no parameters. The Soul is connected to the Source; a little piece of Universe deep within us. It is connected to the stars, to the galaxies, to the infinite energy within each and every one of us. There is no beginning, there is no end. The Soul is the pure energy that makes us who we truly are.

The mind will continue to chatter but the Soul will bathe it with peace; with the cool fire of healing beauty. You are beginning to live your life, your Truth, in honour of your Soul. "

Beginning to integrate Ego and Soul

Begin by becoming fully aware of the physical body. Feel its form, its tensions and its peace. Feel the anxiety, feel the peace. Touch each muscle with your conscious mind. As you do so, begin to acknowledge your emotions. Notice how your emotions impact on the physical form. Change nothing with your conscious mind. Simply sense. Notice. Let go.

Take your conscious awareness now towards the inside of the physical body and begin to sense the vibrations of your inner energy as your breath flows upwards through the spine. Begin to guide your focus away from the cerebral outer surface of the brain to its deep epicentre. In doing so, you will immediately detach yourself from the constant flitting of the mind.

The mind is designed to chatter. It works hand in hand with the Ego, looking all the time for ways in which to protect you from fears by either dwelling or distracting or giving a running commentary of the day. It is the nature of your mind to notice changes in your body and in your energies as you enter meditation. This is fine too. Give thanks to your mind for its efforts and allow it to talk as it will at cerebral level, but by guiding your awareness to the deep, violet centre of your brain, you can let these mental processes pass by like ripples on the surface of the deepest lake. Visualise the ripples as thoughts expanding from a single occurrence in our lives. Mind activity is an inevitable course of energy following any event. As predictable as the ripples chasing the daylight, so are the incessant thoughts of the mind.

In order to transcend the mind and reach the level of the Soul, we need to allow our thoughts to dissipate. They can only travel so far. Our thoughts are confined by the boundaries that we allow to be imposed upon us. The mind can only work with what the Ego can understand. This is a very limited concept, but it is what the mind does. However, although it has the shallowest comprehension it is the mind which tends to speak the loudest while the Soul waits in quiet, trusting wisdom. Waiting to be listened to, ready to shine in Truth, whenever we are ready to allow it to guide us along our true path. Do not look for it; simply allow it to come to you. The more you practice, the more receptive and perceptive you will become.

Remember to keep your point of focus at the centre of the brain. Feel the violet energy permeating through the third eye centre. As you breathe awareness into the centre of your brain, imagine you are projecting a violet light outwards through your Third Eye into your spiritual body. You are beginning to connect now with your Soul, with your Inner Truth. Do not try to follow it, simply let it lead you.

Gradually and naturally, allow your physical body to melt into Universal Consciousness. Feel how each cell in your body, every fibre of your physical being is, like your Soul, a fragment of the Universe. Feel your physical body dissipate into the Earth, feel it melt into the song of the birds. Let outside chatter, smells, noises and sounds dance with the body in glorious fusion with the Universe.

There is no space between your Soul and the Source. There is no physical form, no boundaries but simply a fusion of energy in a variety of forms. There is no hierarchy, there is no Ego. There is no right and wrong, no decisions, no linear time. When we allow ourselves to become the pure white light of Universal Consciousness, we can project our own consciousness wherever or whenever we need to, for in these moments of intense awareness, we have transcended the physical, the emotional; we have comforted and released the Ego, we have become our Inner Light.

Stillness of the mind is one of the most precious gifts we can give to the Soul.

Namaste.

"BRING TO ME THE WISDOM OF GRATITUDE"

"How can this be? How can I feel gratitude for a life which has lead me here? I have nothing. I've lost everything. I have no-one. What is there in my life that could bring any kind of gratitude? If the Universe is Love, then how can I be so undeserving?"

"We are not always where we should be. It is a myth to assume that every conscious moment in our earthly life is perfection because it is not. Sometimes in this human world there are victims of circumstance, and circumstance can be painful, cruel and unjust. Bad things do happen to good people.

"Nobody can deny the gravity of such situations or the impact they have on a person and the devastation that can be caused. What we have to strive for on our spiritual journey is to be able to use bad situations to manifest positive outcome somewhere and somehow. We have choices in our life. We can either continue to fall victim to pain and devastation and allow it to pull us downwards into a black spiral of Shadow; or we can gather up the learning from the situation and use this as a starting point for creating something new and positive from the experience.

"This may be something practical like a new career path or a hobby. It may be a new circle of friends or a new partner. Or it may be something deep within ourselves that leads to new understanding, inner strength or a deeper level of spiritual awareness.

"Gratitude is the essence of spiritual enlightenment. It enriches our daily lives when we step away from the material world and begin to live from the level of the Soul. Through finding Gratitude in even the smallest movements of the Universe, we begin to bathe our own lives in Light and become a little more connected to our Soul.

"Feelings thrive on being felt. Feelings and emotions are created by the Ego yet they can be shaped and driven by the Soul if the Ego can be reassured. If you feel no Gratitude within your life then begin by finding Gratitude for the lives of others. This may sound a rather contrary concept as much unhappiness and discontentment stems from a sense of injustice we experience when we compare our lives to those of others. We envy them their possessions, their looks, their families and their companions. This further feeds our depression and lack of Self-worth, which further feeds our envy and resentment and so on. This is one of those situations when the Soul falls short of the Ego if the Ego is left to fend for itself. It is the Ego that wants for these things. It is the Ego which feels cheated when these things do not fall in our way.

"When the Ego feeds our sense of injustice, we are unable to feel any sense of Gratitude in our lives. On the contrary, we grow resentful and weak, and these feelings feed themselves and strive to fulfil and surpass themselves day by day.

"Once we can begin to see that the Ego is merely a two-dimensional mask, then we can start to talk gently to it and guide it away from destructive behaviour towards enlightened bliss. Once we come to recognize and identify the insecurities that lie beneath our sense of injustice, then we can begin to accept a little glimmer of Gratitude into our daily lives, regardless of circumstance.

"Begin to release undesirable feelings by acknowledging them and accepting them into the situation. Without resistance, they have nothing to fight against, nothing to prove. By offering a mental lotus flower to our undesirable feelings they no longer cast a fearful and unpleasant hold over the Soul."

Meditation for Gratitude

Begin your journal with a gesture of Gratitude. Compile a list of all the things in your life for which you can be grateful. At first this may seem impossible task, so begin by being grateful for all the things that are absent from your life. Imagine how life would be if you couldn't use your limbs, couldn't hear the call of the birds, had nothing for shelter or comfort.

Write. Everything that comes into your head, write it down. Aim for ten things, then when you reach ten, aim for twenty. Soon you will see that, however small, there are many ways in which you can feel Gratitude for the Universe. In doing so, you raise your own frequency to that of abundance and satisfaction, which in turn will begin to magnify and attract the same, little step by little step.

This affirmation for the manifestation of Gratitude can be done anywhere in whichever way it feels right for you. You may choose to sit in quiet meditation, or you may prefer to do it outdoors or in another place of your choice.

When I turn my conscious mind towards Gratitude I sense the abundance of joy and love which surround me.

I have Gratitude and joy for the parts of my body that are healthy and vibrant; for the feel of the earth between my toes and the wind in my hair.

I have Gratitude for my senses; beholding the sacred dawn, the richness of sunset, the depth of night at the end of our waking day.

I have Gratitude for the harmony of the Universe, the song of the birds, the sound of my heart and my breath; my life force.

I have Gratitude for the love which can be found in every waking moment of every day.

I have Gratitude for the energy and abundance which I can pour inwards in order to feel the same love and joy pouring outwards back towards me. I have Gratitude for the ebb and flow of love like the turning of the tides, the journey of the moon.

I feel Gratitude for the seasons, for the wind that energizes and the warmth that heals; for the rain that quenches and cools and the sun which nurtures and warms.

I feel Gratitude for the spirit of the Divine, the Universal Consciousness which speaks through my desires and through the choices that I make.

I feel Gratitude for my health and wellbeing and for the people who can help me through times of illness and despair.

I feel Gratitude for this moment of peace for though it is brief it is eternal. It is the slightest whisper of a feather, it is the greatest star; it is the energy that holds present to the future and future to the past.

Namaste.

"BLESS ME WITH THE WISDOM OF FREEDOM"

"What is freedom? Is it the ability to drive alone to the airport and take a plane to anywhere in the world? Is it the opportunity to choose from a string of lovers just because I can? Because I'm not feeling it; I'm not feeling it at all. In fact, the truth is, I've never felt so trapped in all my life. Trapped by my own insecurities about where love could lead. And ironically, the thing I fear most of all is being trapped.

I'm chasing spirals in this vicious cycle of Self-destruction. Why? I don't know. Maybe what I fear most is being alone."

"Spiritual Enlightenment comes when we begin to realise our true purpose here on Earth. Knowing our purpose helps us to understand our behaviour, our emotions and the way in which we respond to daily occurrences in our lives.

"Some of the greatest Shadows we cast upon ourselves come as a result of living in a state of confusion or conflict about who we truly are and what we are truly here to do. We try to fit ourselves into a variety of custom-made boxes hoping that one of them will fit well enough to define a purpose. In so doing, we unwittingly flout our freedom by clamping ourselves tightly into the wrong mould and forbidding ourselves to fly.

"Once we begin to understand ourselves a little better: our Truth begins to surface, and from this renewed understanding of ourselves emerges our true sense of purpose in this incarnation. Realising this process helps us to understand our periods of confusion and uncertainty which build up as a result of our living in conflict with Truth.

"Be like the birds in their joyous flight. Live freely with abandon, but may your abandon always be rooted in a sense of purpose and faith. Soar and rejoice in your freedom, but do so in the knowledge that you are not alone but instead a part of a greater synthesis between humans, animals, sunsets and stars.

"Harness the energy to encompass the Divine, acknowledging with pure faith that we are sparks of consciousness within a perfect and enlightened Universe.

"Thank the Ego for the protection which it serves but trust that from now on it may always be guided by the Soul.

"Bury your feet in the Earth for you never know when you may need them.

"Feel the vitality of the Earth spiralling upwards through your body while the Light of heaven nurtures your Soul from above.

"Remember always that you are a child of the Earth, carrying your own fragment of God within your heart.

"Know this, and your Freedom will follow."

Meditation for the Expression of Freedom

Freedom is our essence; a state reached when we know our purpose, accept our challenges and reach out with Faith towards our future. Fear holds us from experiencing true Freedom and leads us to places where we do not truly belong. This breeds unrest in our heart and shadows us from our Divine Light. When our Shadows lead us, we can fall victim to our fears and fail to fulfil our Truth.

Freedom is feeling happy knowing who you are; Freedom is having respect for your purpose; Freedom is fulfilling your karmic path in this incarnation; Freedom is feeling yourself soar when you are rooted in the Earth

Sit quietly with your hands resting gently on your knees, palms upward then when you are ready, mindfully close your eyes. Bring your awareness in to your sacred space in whichever way feels right for you today and settle quietly into your breath.

When the moment feels right, begin to visualise yourself drawing in the energy of the Earth with each in-breath. Feel it permeating the Sacral Chakra, the Solar Plexus, and upwards into the Heart Centre. Hold the awareness there for a moment before releasing the breath. Repeat this breathing, visualising with each breath that you are becoming more and more attuned to the Earth's frequency. Feel that, with each in breath, you are pulling the green energy of the Earth upwards and into your heart centre. Maintain this cycle of energy breathing for twelve rounds of breath, each time sinking a little deeper into the meditation.

Now, still maintaining this rhythmic flow of breath and earth energy, begin to gently take your awareness towards the very centre of your brain, deep inside. Take a moment to notice and absorb how this feels. With each in-breath, draw your awareness further away from the cerebral surface of the brain and further into its core. If the mind continues to chatter, allow it to do so but maintain your conscious awareness at the epicentre of the brain.

Visualise there a deep violet light. Breathe into this light for twelve rounds of breath, each time sinking a little deeper into the meditation. Gradually bring the green energy of the Earth upwards into this central point of your brain. Feel it merge with the violet light, causing it to glow brighter and more vibrant with each breath. As you breathe out, visualise the light projecting from the centre of your brain through the third eye to a point beyond your physical form. Maintain this flow of energy and breath, each time breathing deeper, drawing more energy from the Earth, and merging it with the spiritual energy of your Third Eye Chakra.

When the time feels right for you, allow a bright star to form in your visualisation in line with your third eye. As you breathe out, project your breath and your consciousness through the third eye and into this star. With each out-breath, see and feel the star becoming bigger and more vibrant. Maintain this cycle of energy transformation and exchange, drawing upwards from the Earth and merging with the celestial energies of higher consciousness.

Now, as you project outwards towards this star, visualise the white light of your Crown Chakra becoming one with the light from the star. Stay with this beautiful cycle of breath and energy exchange for as long as it feels comfortable and right. If the mind chatter begins, just let it do so without acknowledgement. Focus on the exchange and flow of earthly and celestial energies which you are creating and shaping through your breathing.

When you are ready, raise your arms out to your side, palms facing forwards, as though embracing the sun. Lift the chest and smile with your very essence. Feel the celestial white light of the star you have created bathe you in mind, body and Soul as you breathe out and connect once more with the Earth beneath you.

Allow the sense of true Freedom to come to you. Feel the sense of security and nurturing as you feed from the Earth, and as the Earth, in turn, nurtures and cocoons your physical form.

Feel the sense of boundless soaring as you project your consciousness into the stars. Sense the enormity of Universal Consciousness as it fuses with your own.

Either out loud or in your mind, state this mantra now, three times:

> I am safe.

> I am nurtured.

I am true to my purpose.

I am the earth. I am the stars. I am the Universe.

I am Freedom.

When you are ready, gradually bring your palms together to meet at the heart centre in prayer position. Place the thumbs against the breastbone and feel your heart pulsating with an abundance of earthly and celestial energy as you release the mantra with gratitude. Gently let go of the visualisation, knowing that you can return to it in consciousness any time you wish.

Give gratitude for this moment of true Freedom and know that, whatever your situation and circumstance, you can return any time you wish. Remain for as long as feels right for you. When you are ready, gradually bring yourself away from the meditation, making sure you ground thoroughly.

Namaste

"IGNITE WITHIN ME THE FIRE OF COURAGE"

"The pounding of my own heart in the dead of night when the rest of the world is suspended in sleep; ghosts of discourse weaving echoes of dread between the Shadows of my mind while the rest of the world is in peace...I fear the sound of my own life more than I fear life itself."

"I will tell you a story of Courage. In winter, the tiny, exquisitely formed Monarch butterfly flies unerringly for thousands of unknown miles, to migrate from the hostile Canadian winter to the warmth of the Mexican mountains.

"How can this gossamer being travel such an immense and volatile distance on such fragile wings? The challenge seems impossible, yet the Monarch journeys with effortless grace and absolute faith towards its distant destination, guided by an innate knowledge - its gnosis - of the journey upon which it must embark.

"Embrace your Shadows for they will bear witness to your Courage.

"Relying on the Ego to lead and to make choices means our Shadows are both satisfied and repressed. Sensual pursuits become Selfish desires, driven by secret messages from places deep within our psyche. We cover up hurt, seek revenge on others through the Shadows' Self-gratifying, Self-fulfilling ways.

"Facing Shadows takes great Courage. Sometimes in order to reach them, we have to allow the Ego to lead us through its own journey where Truth is never allowed to shine. Sometimes we need the

Ego to take us right to the depths of our darkness in order to meet it face on.

"You may shock yourself. You may feel anger and despair. You may find yourself in damaging relationships and circumstances as you being to penetrate the walls around the deepest Shadows of your psyche.

"But Shadows are negative imprints of your Truth. Do not try to erase the Shadow. Do not shun or taunt the Shadow.

"Have Courage. Take each Shadow gently by the hand. They are part of your complete Truth, like the dark side of the moon; the unseen breath of night. Have Courage, and they will lead you to your enlightened Self, for in order for a Shadow to form, there must first of all be Light.

"Only when we discover our Shadows, only when we find the Courage to take them into a dance of love, joy and acceptance do we realize the power, the strength, the beauty and the Truth of our Inner Light.

"When we are enlightened, we live once more from the Soul and every choice we make, every path we follow is the right one for us, for it is made with love. Love for the Self, love for others, love for the beauty of nature and gratitude for her earthly gifts. A path may be unfamiliar and unexpected, but it will always be well lit.

"When we embrace the energy around us, it opens us up to the abundance that comes from living in Truth from the Soul. The glory of life's myriad opportunities begins to reveal itself before us and we can walk into our tasks and challenges with Courage and peace. We begin to embrace our conflicts with grace as our Truth begins to transcend the Ego.

"Like the Monarch, we too can make courageous decisions for the good of ourselves and of others by setting free the boundaries of doubt, resistance and fear. As we do so, we take to the air, moving in a dance of effortless communication. Be like the butterfly: graceful and lithe, yet rooted in Courage. "

Walking Meditation for building Courage

To truly see, we first have to learn how to look; but before we can really look, we first have to forget how to see.

So much of what we see is a manifestation of dreams, wishes, hopes, distortions and expectations. So much of what we perceive is guided by the Ego. We need to learn to cast aside these preconceptions about the world around us and reset the lens.

When we forget how to see, we begin to notice. Feel the wash of the tide rippling into your heart then step away from the sound of the pebbles being pulled by the tide, hearing only instead the essence of the sound without name; light without direction. Not as things but simply as patterns of light, form and energy.

Once we lose our preconceived ideas about how the world should look, once our surroundings cease to be a series of connected and independent objects becoming instead a fusion of colour, pattern, rhythm and light, then we can begin to truly LOOK.

Not for objects, for these belong in the preconceived standardized material surface world. Instead, we start to look for details of wonder: a constellation forming within a lake; the synchronicity of a flock of birds moving as one to the rhythm of the Universe. The droplets of sunrise placed with exquisite precision along the finest gossamer web.

Begin to see the world with your Soul; the source of wisdom, intuition and Courage within each and every one of us where true freedom sits ready to transcend the Ego like a flock of birds rising from the shores.

I breathe. I live. I am.

Courage is gentleness; Courage is peace.

Namaste.

"INSTILL WITHIN ME THE GIFT OF BALANCE"

"Why do you come to me with talk of spirituality and Soul? I have nothing to show for a Soul; spirituality brings nothing to the likes of me. My mind is taunted and restless; I am dissatisfied with the world and saddened to the core by injustice and cruelty which surrounds us. The spiritual path is a gift for the chosen few: those who can rise gracefully above unrest and remain unmoved by the taunts of temptation to be driven by lust and material wanting. I am nothing more than an abused body

and a tortured, cynical mind. The spiritual path has no place for my footprints to fall."

"You can learn to find Balance in your life. Touch, breathe, live from the Source, but remember that your feet sink into this Earth each day when you walk and that it is the cool breath of scented air and the warm radiance of the sun which keeps your body alive and full of vitality.

"Maintain great connection with the Universe beyond, fuse with the Source and become the creator within your own creation, but root yourself firmly as the tree grounds its roots within the Earth, for it is within the Earth herself that the essence of the Divine Source lies. We do not need to seek it for it surrounds us every day.

"Connection and fusion with the Source need not be an act of great mystery and divine faith, but an adjustment of love and attitude within our current life. Nothing needs to change in this life, yet with a small shift in energy and consciousness, the entire Universe can shift according to our Soul's intentions.

"Enlightenment should not elevate or isolate, but rather enrich a life already being lived. We must create space within our lives to encompass fear and security; happiness and sorrow; yearning and satisfaction, and the immense spectrum of feelings in between.

"Within every chaos there is a point of perfect balance. Balance of molecules within a single cell right through to the balance of activity and energy in the Universe. Our chaos may be the vital component which creates balance in a wider sphere of our lives. Like concentric circles, our lives unfold on many layers. The complete whole of a life lived and died is only one flicker of existence within a Universe where our life plays a fragmentary role in maintaining balance on a different sphere of consciousness.

"In the pursuit of Spiritual Enlightenment, there is a tendency to focus on higher energies and to endeavour to live from a purely spiritual level. However, the spiritual journey began long before our earthly lives began, and will continue to evolve and grow long after our earthly lives are over. Whilst we are here on planet Earth, it is important to maintain solidarity within ourselves. As human beings, we need to acknowledge and serve the physical, the sensual, and the social as completely as we serve the spiritual aspects of our existence. To focus entirely on one area would throw us out of balance, both energetically and in our daily experiences.

"Balance is the key to a harmonious and joyful life. When we open and nurture each level of our consciousness, we gently remove any power of destruction. When we open our compassion for humanity, we will cease to be affected by disturbances in our personal relationships. When we touch awareness with higher energies, there will be no shame or degradation in sensual pleasure.

"Root your feet in the Earth but stretch your Soul to the Stars."

Meditation for finding Balance

Within each one of us is a deep energy which connects our past to our present, our future to our birth, our Truth to our hearts. This energy is the Source of the Universe, the Source of life itself.

As we evolve spiritually, we naturally become more aware of higher energies. However, it is possible to focus so much on these and to lose touch with the sensual, earthly energies which drive us in our daily lives.

Chakra balancing both reflects and guides our higher energies, expands our spiritual awareness and raises the frequencies of higher consciousness. But it also attunes our senses to the energy and spirit of the earth, and to that of the people with whom we share it.

As we tune our awareness into the Root Chakra at the very base of the spine, we attune ourselves with the basic needs, drives and power of the physical body. It expresses our human need for the physical, the sensual and the strength of being a human body. Breathe awareness into this Chakra, and as you do so, visualise a rich, vibrant red engulfing the physical form. Although this colour is strong, bold and courageous, feel also a sense of balance and gentleness as it connects you deeply into the Earth.

Moving up slightly to the Sacral Chakra associated with the colour orange, we begin to attune ourselves to the power of social contact, the relationships we nurture and the myriad emotions which we experience. It expresses our human need for the emotional and the social, the warmth of shared experience, laughter and the joy of being a human spirit. As you breathe into this Chakra, visualise a warm, gentle orange light, flowing through your body, bringing with it a sense of balance, peace and vitality.

Move the awareness upwards now into the Solar Plexus, visualising as you do so a vibrant yellow energy. Focussing our awareness here and aligning this energy helps us to focus on the power of the mind and enables the mental body to work in collaboration and harmony with both the physical and the higher, spiritual energies. As you breathe into this Chakra, allow the visualisation become a physical sensation. Feel the warmth and power of the solar plexus energy permeate the physical body, bringing with it an abundance of vital energy and a sense of radiance and joy and begin within you the cycle of receiving and radiating this powerful life force.

Moving upwards into the area of the chest, we come to the Heart Centre. As we meditate on this tranquil green energy, we begin to project our awareness beyond the physical body into the subtle bodies of emotion and spirit. This energy is Universal Compassion, projecting peace, harmony and love for humanity and the Earth. Visualise yourself surrounded in a gentle green light, which becomes more vibrant with each in-breath. Feel the sense of nurturing, serenity and peace which it creates within you, and as you breathe out, know that you are radiating universal love and peace offering to those around you and to the sacred Earth which holds us here in this moment.

Now with this awareness for human compassion, we can begin to tune our awareness in to the higher Chakras which connect us to our ethereal and celestial bodies. The Throat Chakra, associated with the colour blue, is our key to communication with others and with ourselves. Spend as long as you need to fuse your conscious awareness to the energy of this Chakra, focussing each time on pure blue light, the colour of sapphires. This Chakra can easily become blocked, as we fail to speak our Truth for fear of going against social expectations or veering from the path upon which we feel safe. As you breathe into this Chakra, focus first on the physical body, asking neck, shoulders and throat to relax. As you breathe out, do so with a soft humming sound, feeling a gentle vibration on the lips. This opens the throat, allowing the energy in the Throat Chakra to vibrate and flow freely. Continue for as long as feels right for you, each time allowing the sensation of vibrant blue light flow through you, unlocking with each out breath, another tiny layer of your Truth.

Raise the awareness now to the Third Eye Chakra, which is about spiritual communication and connection with the Higher Self. It is the energy centre of perception and Gnosis - that deep knowledge that we possess within the Soul, the gift of wisdom which dwells within each of us. Begin by focussing your awareness on the space between the eyebrows, then as you start to breathe, guide this awareness towards the very centre of your brain, deep within the physical form, away from the constant monitoring of the outer layers of the brain. Allow a pool of violet light to form in your visualisation and at the same time, consciously give yourself permission to become receptive to the messages of the world around you, to the energy of others, and to the places where your energy might be needed. Sit within the wisdom of this indigo light for as long as you need. Allow your sixth sense to speak. Be open; have faith. Listen.

When you are completely ready, take your awareness to the Crown Chakra at the crown of the head. The violet light of this Chakra knows no boundaries between our physical body and the Source of

Universal Consciousness. When we truly open the Crown Chakra we become pure Light. We become our Ultimate Truth; we transcend the physical, the mental and the astral. Linear time ceases to exist; we become past, present, future and beyond. We discover eternity. We become the Source. As you breathe into the Crown Chakra, take your awareness to the area just above the head, away from the confines of the physical form. As you focus on this violet light, feel the physical body become ethereal as it dissipates into the energy of the aura and beyond. Feel the connection; feel the boundless unity with the Universe. Become your True Self, if only for a fragment of a second.

Sit with this sense of growing spiritual bliss, and as you do so, visualise the light of the seven Chakras fusing around you into the pure white light of Spirit. Cleansing, healing, enlightening. Remain for as long as feels right for you.

When you are ready, gradually bring yourself away from the meditation, making sure you ground thoroughly.

Namaste.

"GUIDE ME SO THAT I MIGHT FIND TRUTH"

"I have no idea who I am anymore. I'm not sure I ever did. Sometimes I lie awake at night and count the moments I allowed to slip me by and I wonder why I never appreciated them when I had them. I think about places in the world where I felt alive for a while...and I wonder why I am not there now. I think about the people who have come and gone from my life and I wonder why some of them have disappeared...and why others have remained. Is my purpose in life really to spend days working overtime in a job that means nothing to me, and evenings in a bleak spiral of mere existence? There are things I used to enjoy doing when I was younger,

but what's the point in that? It's not going to change things, and pleasure alone won't pay the bills."

"Let me speak to you about Truth. Although we are of the stars, we are not yet in the stars. Find solidarity in the knowledge that your presence on this earth and in this time is not without reason or intention.

"We transform with the waves into the beings we will become, but our true purpose on Earth is yet to be discovered. Be true to your energies for this will become your purpose in this world. Your planetary existence is fleeting - but it is also real.

"Feel, with all that you have, the wet sand beneath your toes and know that it embodies your spirit. Wrap starlight in your hair and wash your body in the light of the moon, but remember you are also within this Earth: fed with cosmic energy, held upright by the energetic forces of nature.

"This planet holds you for as long as you are here. Maybe you will return in form one day, maybe you won't. But stay with the Earth energy in your marrow for it is a beautiful and essential place to be.

"Everywhere you go on earth there are spiritual metaphors to be found in nature. Every intricate twist speaks of a lesson to be learned, an experience to be gained, an emotion to be explored. Learn from spiritual metaphors but learn also to laugh, love and live with abandon and spirit.

"No truth can control the mind other than that of your Soul. No other can dictate your being. If we are to access the deep Truth of Universal Consciousness at the essence of the Soul, then we need to integrate the Shadow into the Ego. We are all enlightened beings, incarnated with faith, trust, Gnosis and unconditional love but sometimes mortality carves Shadows on the Soul. So often we fall into our predicted pattern of behaviour or make choices from the Ego alone. So often we consider and re-consider without realizing that the answer lies within our Soul. The answer is Truth; we are our Truth.

"We over-think so many of our choices; we force ourselves into situations and definitions which fit the Ego alone. Creatures of nature have no Ego. They are guided by Gnosis alone. They know the way to run, they know where to find fulfilment; they know where to begin and they know when to end. Instinctively the bee is drawn to the flower wherein the pollen lies. The bird knows her true song. Let Truth be your guide and you too will live true to the wisdom of your Gnostic Soul."

Finding your Truth

With every Shadow we create, our Ego lays another layer of dishonesty over our light. Shadows cause us to live apart from our Inner Truth, denying ourselves the love, the trust, the reality that we deserve. Many years' worth of Shadows can haunt the Truth of our Soul. Maybe we have become strangers to ourselves. We need to rediscover the person who we are inside, to reconnect with our enlightened Self. Honouring our Truth leads us onto our path of Light: a place in which we know instinctively which way to go; a place in which opportunities will reveal themselves to us because we are able to notice the things that we need.

Maybe you haven't seen your True Self for many, many years. Maybe you never have.

This exercise is not about going within, but about projecting outwards and creating a positive image of the Self. Living in Truth means demonstrating the Self through your words, actions, work, relationships and pastimes, therefore it makes sense to unearth it in a manner that allows you to show it to the world with confidence, pride and most importantly, with love. At first it might feel unsettling to discover and share aspects of your Truth. Maybe there are parts of yourself which you have been concealing or hiding from for a long time.

Expressing your Truth can be a positive and uplifting experience. It is the beauteous and bountiful reward for psychological and emotional clearing. Often our feelings of frustration, dissatisfaction, uncertainty and depression stem from the fact that we are, often without conscious awareness, denying our Truth. We are turning away from our own natural flow of energy in order to struggle along the path of somebody else's dreams.

When we live in Truth we find ourselves on a stream of consciousness that leads us towards opportunities, meetings, situations which fit us, and therefore which bring us the most genuine pleasure and satisfaction, not from the Ego, but from the Soul.

Your key to opening the gateway to Truth will be your journal. Begin by writing your name. Beside it write the first word that comes to you. Next write a list of your dreams and aspirations. If you were the only being in existence, what would you do? Write all the things that you love, all the places you would like to go; all the things that you yearn to experience.

Gather pictures of the things that please you, excite you and appeal to you. Remember that at this moment, this is your journal of Truth and discovery. Fill it with whatever makes YOU happy.

Honestly.

If it feels right for you, begin to use your journal to record and reflect upon events of the day. Explore happenings, interactions, feelings, reactions, reactions to your Self…

There are no obligations, you may find many things already present in your life, you may find very few. Bring a sense of pride and awareness into your exploration.

Find ways of integrating these things into your life. It may be that you begin new activities, maybe casting others aside in favour. It may be that new relationships are needed, that new places in the world are discovered.

An entirely new world and culture can be discovered on the doorstep of your own town. It is not about physical geography but also about spiritual distance from the Self.

As we journey closer to our Truth we need to remember that this Truth is challenged by Ego for the Ego believes there is a reason to keep it away. In so doing there will be Shadows and we need to be prepared to meet them and work with them in order to move them aside.

Remain grounded; there are things in life that cannot be forfeited. However, in acknowledging and knowing who you truly are, your path will henceforth be lit by the Light of your Soul.

"SPEAK TO ME OF ABUNDANCE"

"Everything I once had is gone. All that I yearn for is given to another; everything I work towards is snatched away; everything I have borrowed, I am unable to return. I am wandering blindly, tripping over the bones of my derelict life."

"You have the gift of Freedom beneath your feet - if you will only seek the Courage to breathe.

"You have the fire of Passion burning in your heart - if you will only seek the Honour to let go.

"You have the breath of Truth dancing within your Soul - if you will only seek the Faith to listen.

"You have the Gift of every moment of the day within you: the dance of your body, the energy of your mind, the Wisdom of your heart, the Universal Consciousness which seeks its path within your Soul.

"You have the Gift of Gnosis: a deep knowledge of what the message entails; what is needed of you tonight.

"Have no thoughts but those which are sent in Spirit from beyond the stars, from the Divine Source of Inspiration.

"Return in consciousness to the roots of your existence; feel Divine Consciousness within your Soul: Feel. Listen. Become."

Walking Meditation for the Realisation of Abundance

Abundance surrounds us in every waking day and in every starlit night. Recognizing the abundance in our lives goes hand in hand with the acceptance of gratitude.

It takes courage step away from daily materialism, and to recognize and accept spiritual abundance into our lives. But when you begin to do so, you will be allowing the greatest source of abundance to enter your conscious mind.

The best place to practise this meditation is on top of a hill or in an open space where you can look beyond the horizon.

Focus your eyes gently there for a few breaths and then when it feels right, begin to turn your attention inwards towards your sacred space. By going within yourself mentally, you immediately begin to expand and project yourself outwards spiritually.

With each in-breath, guide your consciousness a little deeper towards your Sacred Space within. Simply observe the natural flow of your energy as it blends more and more with the natural rhythms of the Earth with each breath you take.

Now, begin to breathe into your root Chakra and feel your feet sink into the ground beneath you. Feel yourself merging with the Earth and becoming unified with her healing, vital energy.

Slowly draw that awareness upwards through the Svadhistana Chakra, using the flow of your breath to begin synchronising your feelings and your emotions to the rhythm of the Earth. Just allow it to settle.

Gently let the warm vibrant energy of the sun draw into your Solar Plexus. Visualise and feel this golden energy expanding around you and within you. Feel it spiralling gently within you, feeding your body with vitality and strength; feeding your Soul with power and resilience.

Now focus your awareness on your Heart Centre and visualize a healing green light embracing the Earth around you. Feel it blending into the trees, feel it moving the grass in a dance of Universal Love. Feel the song of the birds, the melodies of Nature, the pull of the waves on the shore. Feel with each breath a growing sense of freedom, a growing sense of love. Feel the energy of your Heart Centre becoming one with the natural rhythm of the Earth as you embrace its nurturing presence.

Moving your awareness upwards once more, begin to open the Throat Chakra to become the song of the Earth. Take a deep, gentle breath in then as you breathe out chant the mantra *Om*. Feel the energy of this sound resounding and vibrating through every cell of the physical body, aligning your frequency to the natural vibrations of the Earth. Feel it resonating within the spiritual body, expanding outwards and merging into the Universe

As you draw your awareness now through the Third Eye, begin to project your consciousness outwards to the galaxies beyond. Fuse your consciousness to the most distant of stars, in the understanding that you are one and the same energy, and although you exist in different times, you also exist simultaneously.

Stand in balance. Merge into the sensual Earth. Connect with the Divine Source.

Now open your eyes once more and, maintaining this sense of balance and inner connection, draw your focus once more to the horizon. This is as far as the physical body can take us. Now look above and take your Soul to the stars. Know that wherever you are in the world you are always standing on the edge of a boundless universe. Billions and billions of miles of harmony and peace surround you. Myriad lifetimes become your past, your present and your future. Wherever you are on Earth, wherever you are in your lifetime, you will always be that boundless, spiritual Universe.

Space and Consciousness abound.

Remain for as long as feels right for you. When you are ready, gradually bring yourself away from the meditation, making sure you ground thoroughly.

Namaste.

"GUIDE ME TOWARDS ACCEPTANCE"

"I am sick to the heart of people telling me that everything is as it should be; that all is perfect in this moment. Such smug arrogance, when my mind is in shreds, my body is failing and my Soul is merely a Shadow of a memory. How can that be true for someone who is in pain and dying through no fault of their own? How can that be true for someone who has lost everything and everyone closest to his heart?"

"I will show you a story of Acceptance. Look above and around you at the clouds. Everybody perceives something different in the same cloud formations. Some may see a dragon, yet another may see an ocean. What becomes the hand of a savage for one becomes for another a lotus flower. Every situation in our life is like the cloud patterns: ever changing, ever dependent on perception.

"If one hundred people bear witness to a life event, one hundred versions of the same story will be told. There is no beginning and no end, no truth but the eternal Truth, the Sacred Truth of the Divine Source. Much of what we create and perceive in this life comes from our own perceptions within ourselves.

"Make peace with your own Soul, find your own Light of truth within, and your perceptions will be full of hope, courage, faith and power. Trust in the Universe, trust within your Soul, trust between the Souls of others, and you will always find a lotus flower.

"When you shield your inner Light through Shadows of fear, anger, frustration and angst, then you will only ever see the savage. Have faith in the fluidity of change: as the clouds move through the sky, ever changing, so we can move through our lives and our interactions, ever fluid, ever changing. Some clouds converge and join and evolve into new and spectacular forms, moving together, moving apart, joining energies and drifting asunder to form their own dance. Others dissipate gradually into thinner and thinner air…until there is nothing left of their physical presence in the ether.

"So we lead our lives here on Earth. Perceptions of the Ego can halt the dance and draw a dragon fist; perceptions of the Soul bring a lotus flower of peace, ever dancing, ever evolving; ever changing with Acceptance, faith and love."

Mindfulness Exercise for Acceptance

With every situation which comes to challenge us, we need to consciously take root for a while in order to understand it from every angle, perceive it in every possible guise. We need to ground ourselves in the present day and observe what is happening around is – and within us – and to watch the movement unfold. We need to allow the energy and the gravity of the situation to be absorbed into our minds and bodies so that we provide our Soul with the space it needs in order to listen and to act.

Too often, the Ego makes its own perceptions and forces the mind to act immediately before we have allowed any time to feel and absorb. Too often, we allow our Shadows to dictate the next move when often we need to wait a while to find what our Light will reveal and what our Soul needs to learn.

Like the roots of the tree, we need to journey deep below the surface to stand strongly in the storm, and to flourish and stretch beyond the limitations of the Ego.

Often we expect immediate resolution and act in haste because our Ego tells us we should. Yet always what we need are peace and space and a little human time to adjust ourselves to the situation and to allow it to fully reveal itself before any action can be taken.

Accepting a challenging situation does not justify wrong doings, or nullify hurt. It simply means allowing ourselves time so that we can better comprehend its role in our lives and to find the best course of action. Sometimes, from a seemingly bad situation, things can happen for the benefit of our highest good. Uncertainties become clear, lessons are learned; new opportunities come our way.

The Shadow of Acceptance is resistance. Resistance creates internal struggle and never allows us to see anything but the dragon in the clouds. In taking time to exercise Acceptance within ourselves, we remove the internal struggle for there is no tempest against which we must battle in blindness. In removing resistance, we allow a path for Light to flow. Light to guide our way; Light from our own Soul. Contemplate this as you meditate on the following affirmations, in whichever way feels right for you:

Acceptance does not mean forever.

Acceptance is the gateway to change.

Acceptance is the key to freedom.

Freedom opens the door to the Light.

Light reveals answers with clarity and conviction.

I am Light, therefore all answers lie within me.

Remain for as long as feels right for you. When you are ready, gradually bring yourself away from the meditation, making sure you ground thoroughly.

Namaste.

"BATHE ME IN THE BLISS OF FORGIVENESS"

"I'm tired of hearing, reading, being told that every hurt and every unfortunate situation is a result of my own failings; that every negative action, every cruelty, every loss is a reflection of something dark within myself. How can one's own shortcomings be responsible for the torture of innocents at the hands of religious extremists; for the physical and emotional ruin inflicted by violation, abuse and rape? How can a child be responsible for their own neglect and abuse? How can I

humanly forgive someone who has caused such horrific wounds to my mind, body and spirit while they walk free and untouched? If this is what is expected of me, then I shall never be able to walk the spiritual path."

"There are times when other people choose to hurt us, sometimes with profound intent. They can act in ways that are malicious, vicious and cruel, inflicting terrible damage on good, innocent people. Victims of such hurt and abuse are not always responsible for the deep, unhealed wounds inflicted upon them in body, mind or spirit. When this happens, the concept of Forgiveness is virtually impossible to conceive for it implies that the wounds have been healed and that the hurtful actions and behaviour have been condoned. Although often we allow ourselves to be hurt by others through our own manifestations and fears, we cannot and should not try to make ourselves responsible for every hurt another person causes to us, because it is not always within our control to do so. A child fallen victim to abuse; an innocent citizen persecuted for their faith; a defenceless lover attacked by their partner; sometimes we are powerless against other people's actions, and to forgive, to say it is past, does seem unjust and wrong somehow. We should not always be expected to simply forgive the persecutor or the inflictor of pain and move on in our lives, because sometimes this is simply too much to ask.

"However, what we do need to do is find a means of healing the wounds in our own mind, body and spirit in order to develop our spiritual selves more deeply from the experience and to begin living once again in joy and Light. Forgiveness does not mean condoning or allowing something to not matter anymore. Forgiveness means release. It is the ability to fall back into the flow of life with mindfulness and awareness so that we can fully live our lives in the present without being governed by memories or dreams; so that our chosen memories can rest in the palms of our hands like stardust that can as easily be blown away as it can be nurtured, cherished and loved.

"We can begin to do this by developing a conscious and profound love for the Soul. Gradually, with dedication and practice, over the course of time we can learn to adapt and control our responses to other people's actions, mistakes and misguidance in ways which will minimize our own suffering as much as possible. But we cannot and should not endeavour to perceive ourselves solely as instruments of blame for the wrongdoings of others. To do so would allow terrible hurts; to condone acts against love.

"Sometimes though, repeated patterns of hurt, loneliness and shame do indicate a subconscious reflection of our own hidden Shadows. Often enough we use the Ego to mask the Shadows of our most undesirable traits and flaws from our conscious awareness. However, on a deeper level, these Shadow elements of the Self crave acknowledgment and healing and so, unwittingly, we call them into the forefront of our lives in the form of other people. For example, through our subconscious fear, we may become possessive and perceive aloneness as neglect; through our masked insecurities we may learn to idolize a disinterested lover; through our embedded Self-loathing we will subject ourselves to many forms of abuse. To consciously recognise and address our Shadows directly is a dangerous task from which the Ego works incredibly hard to protect us, so instead, it enables us to safely nurture or chastise our Shadows in whichever way we choose as they present themselves to us through the behaviour and responses of others.

"As we begin to meet our Shadows, much forgiveness needs to take place within our own Self in order to begin healing. One of the most powerful Shadows we need to work with inside ourselves is fear - and yet this is the hardest of all to release. Why do we hold so tightly onto fear as though our very lives depended on it? Maybe it is because we are afraid of what it might do to us if we don't. We trap our fear in a box and try to keep it hidden in the depths of the deepest, darkest Shadow, lest it should show itself in its fullness and entirety. To lose fear, you must release it from this box. But in order to let it out of its box, you must first of all acknowledge that it exists. When we begin to forgive and release our own fear, we begin to move our journey forward, tiny step by tiny step. With lightness of mind, we can move onwards in our Soul.

"Conflict within relationships can be an active, creative energetic force. However, as with all energetic forces, we have to learn to channel it in a safe and nurturing way which will be beneficial to us from deep within. With conflicts come opportunities for integrity to unfold. As we begin to know ourselves on a deeper level, we begin to see what we can learn from various situations. We begin to recognise the mask that hides the Shadow and then we can begin to unearth the Shadow itself. A Shadow is not an imprint. It can be released when we are ready, integrated into Light when we feel safe to let go.

"Eventually, we become agents of choice and we learn to adapt and control our responses. We can learn from other people's errors and misguidance. We can to learn to develop ways to protect our Light and Soul from the damage that could potentially be caused and created by other people's injuries. We can learn to reflect upon ourselves through experiences. We can learn from the ways others behave around and towards us but we should never presume sole responsibility for the distribution of hurt. Protect your spirit. Surround your Soul in love. As we build on our Self-belief we can build up a great strength of spirit to gradually deflect negativity and unwanted behaviour back to its source. We can refuse to accept it.

"Reflect upon your relationships past and present. Reflect with gratitude upon the wisdom and learning they have brought you. Reflect with gratitude for the opportunities and journeys which may have come about as a result. Reflect upon the insight into your own Shadows which your relationships might have begun to reveal. During the course of our lives we will all be teachers and we will all be students of wisdom.

"Forgiveness makes way for the flow of Universal Energy. In holding onto old memories and contriving them to guide our way, we form psychic boundaries in the path of conscious flow. We cannot attract those whom we need to attract. We can truly live if we can release and set ourselves free to absorb the natural flow of divinity.

"Forgiveness is releasing the Soul from the clutches of the Ego so that it can grow and shine in Light and love."

Gesture of Forgiveness

For each memory or preoccupation that is holding you back, take a piece of paper and write it down. Imagine these are the petals of your beautiful, perfect lotus flower. On each paper petal, write down the person, the action, the regret, whatever it may be from the past – or from the possible future – that is putting a barricade, however small or large, in the path of your natural flow. Write as much or as little as you need. One word may suffice for some; pages for another. As you begin, you will find that more and more obstacles begin to pour out of you. Keep writing.

Some memories are so beautiful and so precious that you will always keep them. Write them too. They too will have their work to fulfil today.

When you have finished, surround yourself with all these pieces of paper; all these memories and fears and wishes and regrets which have been clogging up your energetic field.

Now it is time to sort through these memories and feelings and thoughts.

Those beautiful, sacred and special memories that you wish to keep forever, take these to one side and lay them with dedication and care into a place where they can be safely kept: a box, a notebook, a drawer. Bless them, thank them then put them away for cherished safekeeping.

Now it is time to release the rest of these memories.

Release them with gentleness and peace. Bless them with gratitude, for every experience brings a lesson, and every lesson brings an opportunity for change. In releasing the past and the fears of the future, we open ourselves to receive and channel energy and messages that we need now in the present moment allowing us to manifest truth and find our own Light within our lives.

Release them one by one with mindfulness and love. Watch them float away on a current, or tie them to a balloon and watch them float away, or see them curl and vanish into flames, then return to the Sacred Space within yourself in whichever way feels right for you today.

Feel that connection with the Earth, hear the sounds around you and sense your connection with the air. As you do so, feel the connection with your Higher Self.

Focus on your Heart Centre and bring to your awareness a gentle sense of green light. Imagine now that you are breathing in this pure, gentle green light. This is the light of protection. Ground yourself in the sensation of this light. Then, when it feels right for you, bring your awareness back into your physical body.

Today you have opened up and begun to clear the way for new experiences and new opportunities to come into your path. With clarity and lightness of spirit, continue your day with gratitude for the refreshing, vibrant joy of Forgiveness and release.

Namaste.

"TEACH ME TO HAVE FAITH"

"What if there is no 'right answer'? What if life really is just an infinite series of options, any of which could be taken on board; any of which could lead to destruction?"

"Life is eternal. We may be reincarnated into new form, but all exists together because we are one and the same energy regardless of human past or present. And the enlightened Soul is constant within each and every one of us because we are the Source and the Source is within us all. Every waking moment, every second of sleep, every birth and death, and cycle of earthly life is simply a continuum of the Source which is each of us at once and together.

"Everything in life has two forces: day and night, yin and yang, fire and water, air and earth. Without Shadows, we cannot perfect the dance. Where night meets day, there is the perfect pinnacle of light which bathes the land in dew and touches the wings of eagles with the promise of fire. When day meets night, the heat of the day becomes melting Shadows across the land, turning fire back into earth. Within each moment there is darkness and there is light. As the sky around us fades to black, the light of a billion galaxies glitters above and around us. These immense and distant sources of light, unseen by the light of day become perceptible only through the presence of darkness.

"Even within the Shadows of our mind there is a Light so gentle, so eternal, so certain to be seen if we can only step back and perceive it with the Soul.

"As humans, we have an innate need to understand the world; to attribute cause and effect to everything that goes on around us. Because we understand the way the solar system works, we can let the darkness of night pass us by, for we know with absolute certainty that the darkness will pass; that night will soon become day; that the sun will ignite the earth once more and bless the skies with radiance.

"Were we to approach our own lives with such certainty and connection and understanding of the Soul then we too could pass through the Shadows of our own lives with acceptance and faith, knowing with absolute certainty that the darkness will pass and give way to Light once more.

"See how the birds fly. In perfect synchronicity they take off and land. Their signals are imperceptible yet somehow they know to move in perfect synthesis with one another. There are no false moves, no failed beginnings. Each movement is accomplished, and effortless and taken in perfect harmony.

"They know no conflict of Ego for they live perfectly from within. They are drawn without effort to their destination. They have no concept of doubt or fear. They know only that they must carry out their journey on fragile wings against the harsh and unpredictable earthly elements.

"Yet they are free."

"The birds do not need to be told when spring will come for with each new voyage of the Earth, the spring will follow with inevitable grace and winter will remain but a fossil on the landscape of time.

"Strive instead to be like these birds. For deep within us, within our enlightened Soul, lie the same courage, the same faith, the same synthesis and Gnosis. When we lift the Ego, we turn our Shadows to Light and we too will soar in freedom.

"Let the force of the wind lift you in your flight. May the stars light your way, let the natural rhythm of the Universe dictate your pace and create your dance.

"Follow that which lies in your heart, for this is your Inner Truth which will light your journey with wisdom and faith.

"Honour that which your destiny becomes, for destiny knows itself and dwells within your heart. Be lifted by the power of synthesis. Know with deep and divine faith that no Soul is isolated from the Universe for we are all sparks of the same divine faith which burst into being at the dawn of time.

"Lost cities may lie before and beneath us but it is only in following our hearts and living from the essence of our Soul that these will be rediscovered and unveiled through our acquired wisdom, our constant faith and our innate Gnosis. Life does not happen in a day. It happens all around us. We exist as pure Source yet our destiny is our own."

Meditation for Faith

Sit or lie quietly in a position that is comfortable to you. Rest your hands quietly in your lap and close your eyes. Take your awareness to your breath as you take yourself deeper into your Sacred Self in whichever way feels right for you today.

Allow to form in your mind's eye a perfect, frosty night. The sky is a deepening fusion of indigo and deep turquoise in which a tiny crescent moon glows as brightly as the hidden sun. As the sun sets deeper, the sky darkens to almost blackness, and gradually the full image of the moon begins to emerge as a faint yet perfect imprint in the sky.

Though the exquisite arc of light burns with ever increasing intensity, we now perceive it as merely a part of its entirety. We can learn from this wonder of nature as a metaphor for faith in the Divine and gratitude for earthly bliss.

Breathe in the understanding that what we perceive to be truth in its entirety is only part of a bigger, complete whole. Experiences which we perceive to be finite are a fluid part of a sacred body of consciousness. What we usually perceive as isolated misfortune, events, issues and dilemmas, are part of an integral whole which we cannot perceive until the conditions and situations are so that it is possible for such insight to come to us. It is only when the darkness of night unites with the eternal light of the sun that the full cycle of eternity is revealed.

Now, take your awareness gently away from the moon, and visualise yourself stepping away from your body into the serenity of the Universe. Look upon your body as a tiny kernel of energy around which an infinite stream of pure light revolves, swirls and dances. This light is the energy which you attract and from which you can choose. Sense the boundless nature of this energy; see it dissipate into the stars. Now visualise yourself stepping away from the planet into this golden energy. Visualise the whole planet revolving within the serenity of the Universe. You are so far away you can see it in its entirety; its seas and oceans; its diverse and glorious landscape. Now imagine you can take this planet and nurture it in cupped palms. Feel it rotate within your hands. As you breathe in and out, visualise the air filling the planet, see it expand a little as you inhale, and relax as you exhale.

Now feel yourself moving further away into the realm of the stars.

Om

Feel the vibration of this sacred sound through your physical body; feel the same frequencies holding the Universe together in perfect harmony. Feel the overwhelming sense of peace and unity; feel the boundaries of linear time dissolve as you immerse yourself and diffuse your physical body into the eternal energy of the Divine Source.

Now, when it feels right for you, gently come to visualise again that crescent moon shining in the deep, indigo sky, and know that you too shine out with your own individual Light but that you are the essence of harmony with the infinite and eternal Universe.

Shine your Light in honour and love for the Universe.

Remain for as long as feels right for you. When you are ready, gradually bring yourself away from the meditation, making sure you ground thoroughly.

Namaste.

"ENLIGHTEN ME WITH THE GIFT OF JOY"

"I knew a young boy once, whose life was full of dreams. They fluttered and they danced like fireflies around him, inviting him on the adventure of chase, teasing him with the sweet sting of disappointment and the delicious kernel of success. Everything was exciting; everything was new. There was no such thing as failure, for each unplanned outcome was a new adventure. Minutes were like glorious hours; one day could hold an entire years' worth of emotions and experiences. Now all that

is left of this lissom boy are the charred remains of a spirit and a body so worn by failure that it can barely move to bat a tiresome firefly from his eyes."

"In the pursuit of enlightenment do not turn inside yourself but embrace the life that you are living in here and now and gradually, as you heal your Soul, you will begin to love your life again.

"Divine energy flows through you like a river of inspiration and life. You are Source and every day the Source is to be loved and nurtured. But your place in this life is to be human in your essence. Sensual pleasure is no shallow pursuit, no sign of sin for we are glorious, sensual beings. We breathe, touch, desire and taste sensuousness. Nurturing the body is vital as it is the vehicle of the Soul in our earthly life. Without the body, we could not run, paint, write, create music, speak or listen. The body is here and now. It is, like the Soul, pure energy, which should be nurtured and loved – not only for survival but also for pleasure and Joy.

"Do not isolate the Soul but spread your energy amongst others. Humans are not solitary beings. Though our space is sacred, it is our purpose here on Earth to love, to share, to nurture, to cherish those around us, and to live with joy, abandon, happiness and love. The further we travel in our Soul's journey towards enlightenment through the pleasure and enjoyment of life's gifts, the more Shadows we shed, the more we allow our true Inner Light to radiate within, around and beyond us. Consequently, the higher the frequency of our spiritual energies becomes, the closer our connection with the Source.

"We need sacred time alone to connect with our Higher Self, to mindfully consider the day's events and to consciously manifest our path for the day to come, however we should not expect ourselves to be confined within our spiritual pursuits.

"Allow your energy to radiate from the Source. Bring your Light into the lives of others. Through enlightenment learn again to laugh like a child, to dance with abandon, and to find humour, laughter, Joy and bliss in every waking day.

"Recognise the Shadows in others, and help them to set them aside and walk alongside them on the path of true Light. Be real. Love the energy of your children. Nurture the plants you grow. Respect the food that you cook – and enjoy it! Listen not only to that which your body needs, but also that sensual pleasure which it desires. There is no sin in that, only human adoration and love for the earthly world around us."

Meditation for manifestation and expression of Joy

As we begin to open up and realise our connection to the Source, we can begin to live in its essence as radiant beings of Light once again. Our natural vibrational frequency is raised. The higher our frequency, the better and higher we can attract from the Universe. When we live from a spiritual, soulful level, Joy flows in through peace, through synchronicity, and we become aligned to that higher frequency.

Joy follows acceptance and realisation of abundance. Joy flows when we learn to forgive and to release old, compacted energy. Joy spirals through the physical body as we unite Spirit and Earth. Rejoice in the energy of the day. Open your arms to the sun, be it metaphorically or actually. Spread your palms to allow the warmth to radiate through them into your body. Channel this golden energy through your physical body, feeling it flow like a stream through your veins, and into every cell of your physical form. Allow the sensation of your physical form to dissipate and feel this golden light permeate into your spirit. Lightness of body brings lightness of spirit. Surround your aura with golden energy. Become the light of the sun.

Namaste.

"SOOTHE ME WITH THE GIFT OF PEACE"

"My mind cannot settle. Thoughts and fears race through my head at a rate I cannot even begin to comprehend. My body mimics my mind in a constant, relentless fight against myself and the world. Sleep eludes me for I fight constantly against this internal force that I cannot define and which will never, ever be pacified."

"In striving to fulfil our destiny, we often forget the power of stillness. Sometimes in order to move forward on the right path, or to achieve our desires and deepest dreams, we need to root ourselves in our current situation for a while so that we can truly see.

"Imagine climbing a mountain, pushing ourselves and striving for the pinnacle of our journey; being the best that we can be in the shortest amount of time. We get there, but we miss so much along the way. If we stop halfway, look back on the accomplishments we have achieved already and take in the view, the world around us already takes on a whole new perspective; one of which we were formerly unaware. We see beauty and strength in the landscape around us. We see new and inevitable changes in our journey, spot new paths, see with greater insight the endless opportunities and possibilities spread out before us.

"When we stand still, and survey our world from this new perspective, our bodies begin to connect with our sacred reservoir of inner stillness. We become attuned to our heartbeat, to the life-giving motion of our beautiful breath. We become subtly attuned to the gentle signals within our mind's eye, the tiny nudges of the Soul; the higher mind, guiding us, talking to us, telling us the true way to go.

"When we pursue our goals with one rigid focus, we blindly follow a path which may not even be our own. In standing still we can allow the most significant movements to take place.

"In finding stillness and solidarity during phases of our life journey, we become like a seed head landing within fecund soil. Floating freely on the air it is fey and delightful, full of spirit and abandon, and this is a necessary and nurturing element of being truly alive where we discover the innate ability to laugh and play with childlike and reckless abandon. However, in allowing the seed to land and root occasionally, the plant begins to flourish. It grows more beautiful, more bountiful day by day. In the same way, by grounding ourselves and staying put for a while, we can allow ourselves to flourish within the solidarity of Peace. Peace within the Soul.

"These are not times for making conscious decision or focusing on change, for such decisions are driven by the Ego. Rather, these are times for developing and enriching everything that you already have that makes you who you are, that conspires with your Soul to bring you truth and courage.

"Naturally you will start to develop towards your Inner Truth like a plant leans towards the light. Negative or useless pursuits and energies will shed naturally like autumn leaves, and positivity and life will flourish like new buds in bloom.

"Sometimes in order to move onward, we need first to find solace in the stillness of true Peace."

Candle Meditation for Peace

Sit cross-legged in a comfortable place where you will not be disturbed or distracted. If you need to, you can lean against a chair or against the wall to support the back, but it is important to keep the spine straight if possible in order to allow energy to flow freely up and down the spine.

You may already have a space dedicated to meditation, reflection and prayer, but if this is not the case, then find a space which will become a dedicated corner of solitude for this moment of meditation and Peace.

Place a candle in front of you and as you light it, be mindful of the act of Peace that you are about to offer. Sit quietly, legs crossed, with the backs of your hands resting lightly on your knees. Join the thumb and the forefinger gently together and stretch the remaining three fingers out in front. This gesture is known as the *guyan mudra*. It creates a sense of unity, receptivity and calm within the Self and conveys a gesture of Peace to the world around you.

Maintain a gentle, steady gaze on the flame. Do not stare but instead keep the gaze resting as though your vision is a feather floating on this peaceful pool of light.

Draw your awareness now to your breath and feel the coolness as it draws in through the nose and the warmth of as it glides outwards, cleansing, soothing and healing with each wave of breath.

As you breathe, gradually guide the awareness around the body, touching each point of tension with your consciousness. Breathe into these areas of tension and ask the tension to leave your body as you breathe out.

Feel the space between your eyebrows melting away down the side of your face, sliding away into the ether. Feel the shoulders soften and drop away from the ears. As they do so, notice how the tension from the neck drips away down the spine and into the earth.

Breathe with total mindfulness into each individual vertebra, parting them a little with your consciousness, and breathing healing energy into the spaces in between.

Now, visualise the space between the ears relaxing and opening just a little more with each in-breath that you take. Now, take your awareness to that space, deep inside your brain and as you gaze into the candle flame, feel that your gaze is coming not from your eyes at the front of your face, but from deep within the sacred space at the deepest centre of your brain.

Sit quietly in stillness and maintain the conscious flow of breath. Keep your focus gently on the flame and observe how it sways gently to the dance of the energy in the room around you. Take your gaze to the golden aura around the candle, and as you do so, become aware of your own sacred aura in the Crown Chakra, just above the crown of your head. As you breathe and meditate on the dance of the candle, feel its energy and light permeate your own.

Breathe. Gaze. Absorb. Relax.

Remain here for as long as feels comfortable and right for you. Notice the stillness of your mind and the sense of Peace and softness within your body – a perfect sacred gift to the Soul.

When the moment feels right for you, guide this healing, peaceful energy to a place where it is needed most. This may be a physical place, an emotional place or a spiritual place. It may be within yourself, it may be guided towards another.

Now visualise yourself sitting in stillness and peace within this room. Notice how the vibration of the room has settled and become peaceful in harmony with your own meditation and breathing.

Gently close your eyes now and focus once again on the mudra. Feel the connection between the thumb and forefinger, representing the unity and centring within the Self. Be mindful of your outstretched fingers, sending this gesture of Peace outwards into the world with your consciousness.

Before gently opening your eyes and showing Gratitude for this moment of unity and Peace, allow the following mantra to flow through your conscious awareness:

I am at Peace.

My mind is still.

My body is at rest.

My Soul is at Peace.

My Sacred Truth resonates within me.

I am Peace; Stillness.

Remain for as long as feels right for you. When you are ready, gradually bring yourself away from the meditation, making sure you ground thoroughly.

Om Shanti.

Peace.

Namaste.

"EMPOWER ME WITH RESILENCE"

"The Sanctuary which I bring you now resides in you always. My energy is yours, dwells within you as yours wraps around me. My body may depart but you will find me in other ways. I am the voice inside your mind when you have nowhere else to go. I am the silence in the stars and the fire beneath the earth. You are me, therefore I am you and we together are the Universe and the Universe is us. Soon you will come to understand that the physical body is the vehicle through which your own spark of Consciousness can act with purpose and direction within the human world. When the body dies the Soul in not released or transformed, it simply carries on. Each of us has a journey to be fulfilled. Never give up on your journey. Life is your journey; your destination will call you in when you learn to understand the signs of the Universe.

"Do not expect your journey to be perfect and smooth at all times. If you hit rough terrain, stop still a while and look back on what you have accomplished so far and renegotiate the route. Wherever you are travelling to and wherever you have come from, the journey is your own. You choose the route you take and the provisions you need to guide and sustain you. You choose the food for your Soul. You choose the view you want to see, you establish the perspective from which you wish to view it.

"The moment you begin to allow gratitude into your life, energies will change, fortunes will turn. No matter how bleak, there is always potential for heartfelt gratitude. Gratitude will flow to you, through you and within you.

"When we live from the Soul, when the true Light shines within and around us, our decisions and choices are made in love, with no need to consider our actions or question our motivation.

"When you turn your eyes the setting sun, remember that a new dawn is already growing. As you surrender your body to the light of the setting sun, know with faith that before you begin already the twitching of new beginnings in the pale light of dawn. Behind every closing moment, every death, every ending, a new beginning unfurls. This is not cause and effect, but rather it is the natural and eternal rotation of life and death, of ending and beginning. As we move through our daily lives as human beings of every possible dimension, we too work as a natural cycle of Light and Shadow, fear and courage, confidence and pain. Life is cyclic. It takes the form of concentric circle, ever expanding, ever moving, a constant ebb and flow of positive and negative energy and experience. Our lives unfold with us in the most deliciously malleable way.

"As we look to the coming dawn, we see behind us the remains of the darkness we leave behind. This darkness never ceases to exist for, like the glowing promise of new dawn, its existence is constant.

We see what comes to us from the viewpoint upon which we choose to stand."

Affirmation for Resilience:

Find a place of tranquillity and bring yourself to the Sacred Space within yourself in whichever way feels right for you today. As you breathe, breathe in the knowledge that your inner flame is the Source of all that is creation incarnate.

Feel within your being the strength of universal love, manifest in your actions and thoughts. Return to that place of stillness, for that is the rock which grounds you into the roots of the Earth, made of the stardust which penetrates the core of human existence.

Listen to the messages within your heart as you draw towards this inner flame, for you are the Universe. Know through deep, innate Gnosis that you can return.

All that happens around you and within you is Creation. Breathe in deeply and focus on the inner core as you silently repeat the mantra:

I am safe

I am nurtured

I am humble

I am protection

I am strength

Breathe in the Mantra. Feel the Mantra.

Om: The vibration of the Universe.

Nurture inner stillness. When you find that perfect cave of silence within your Soul, you discover the Source within you. You can listen to the messages you hear in these moments of silence. You become the vibration of the Universe. You become wholeness and completion.

Feel how your connection is such that the exterior of the body is shed and lost within the vibration of Divine Source. Feel that it is not merely a connection but a synthesis of the Self and Divine Energy. Feel that you are a body of pure Light through which strength and resilience form from Love, Truth and Divinity.

Remain for as long as feels right for you. When you are ready, gradually bring yourself away from the meditation, making sure you ground thoroughly.

Namaste.

STANDING IN THE LIGHT OF TRUTH

A man stands on the edge of a cliff, his face to the rising sun. Nobody knows he is there, but he feels the pulse of his own heart and knows at once that he is one with the natural rhythms of the waking day.

Above him and around him, the last stars dissipate into the golden sky, present for eternity yet overwhelmed by the light of the sun. Another new day opens her arms to him. He beholds the sun as it rises before him. He absorbs the energy it brings to the very core of his being.

Let this be the one thing that will drive him onwards today.

Namaste.

ABOUT THE AUTHOR

Rowella James holds a First Class BSc Honours Degree in Psychology and a foundation certificate in Art Therapy. She is also a practicing artist whose paintings are exhibited and sold in England and Europe. Her first book, "Fifteen Ways to Heal the World" was published under the name Lucy Rowella Tibbits.

The majority of my writing is channelled Wisdom from Universal Consciousness. I do not claim to be a guru who lives a perfect life solely by the example of her written word. Rather, I am a child of the Earth with a myriad experiences, a catalogue of human errors and my own array of patterns which still need to be broken.

The words which come to me are often the lessons which I need in my own life. Sometimes I ask for specific guidance and this will be brought to me at the right time. Other times, the message flows through me when it will, sometimes unawares. And so it is my duty and my calling to share this blessed Wisdom with you and pray that it brings Guidance, Faith and Light to your life and those around you.

Rowella James

NOTES AND REFLECTIONS

Printed in Great Britain
by Amazon